Good Food

Written by DeMar Reggier

Illustrated by David Austin Clar

My First
READER

children's press®

A Division of Scholastic Inc.
New York Toronto London Auckland Sydney
Mexico City New Delhi Hong Kong
Danbury, Connecticut

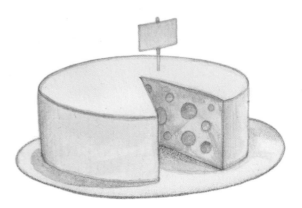

Library of Congress Cataloging-in-Publication Data

Reggier, DeMar, 1928-
  Good food / by DeMar Reggier ; illustrated by David Austin Clar.
      p. cm. — (My first reader)
  Summary: A boy grocery shops for nutritious food with his father, and together they cook dinner for the family.
  ISBN 0-516-24879-0 (lib. bdg.)   0-516-24969-X (pbk.)
  [1. Food habits—Fiction. 2. Grocery shopping—Fiction. 3. Cookery—Fiction.] I. Clar, David Austin, ill. II. Title. III. Series.
  PZ7.R2594Goo 2005
  [E]—dc22
                          2005004021

1 2 3 4 5 6 7 8 9 10 R 14 13 12 11 10 09 08 07 06 05

Note to Parents and Teachers

Once a reader can recognize and identify the 47 words
used to tell this story, he or she will be able to successfully
read the entire book. These 47 words are repeated throughout
the story, so that young readers will be able to recognize
the words easily and understand their meaning.

The 47 words used in this book are:

a	for	like	pick	too
all	get	likes	picks	turkey
beans	gets	looks	please	want
buy	good	make	red	wash
can	greens	milk	says	washes
cheese	I	Mom	shopping	we
cook	it	must	some	with
Dad	kinds	nuts	tastes	
dinner	leafy	of	the	
food	let's	our	tomatoes	

I like shopping for food with Dad.

Dad says we must buy good food.

Dad picks some leafy greens.

I pick some red tomatoes.

Dad likes all kinds of nuts.

I like all kinds of beans.

Dad gets some cheese.

I get some milk.

I want a turkey.
"Can we buy it, please?"

I like shopping with Dad.

"Let's make dinner for Mom," says Dad.

We cook the turkey.

I wash the tomatoes.
Dad washes the greens.

Our dinner looks good.
It tastes good, too!

ABOUT THE AUTHOR

DeMar Reggier lives in Kansas City where she tends a garden planted for butterflies and birds. There is also a shade area for toads, rabbits, and occasional opossums. When she's not writing for children, DeMar enjoys walking her Yorkshire terrier Khory Ires (an anagram for Yorkshire), traveling, listening to jazz, and reading poetry.

ABOUT THE ILLUSTRATOR

David Austin Clar says he can't remember a time when he wasn't drawing. In grade school, he was always the one chosen at holiday time to draw chalk masterpieces on the school blackboard. In addition to his love for art, David enjoys astronomy, photography, music, art history, rare books, cooking, and canoeing. Occasionally his artwork involves collaboration with his wife Corrine, who is an accomplished calligrapher. They live in Rochester, New York, with their three children.